SO, IT'S YOUR FIRST JOB

A QUICK-ISH GUIDE TO NAVIGATING THE WORKING WORLD

Written by Mari Orozco-Onyskin

Illustrated by Brad Onyskin

Copyright © 2025 KASALEARN

www.kasalearn.com

All rights reserved.

The characters and events portrayed in this book are fictitious. Any similarity to real persons, living or dead, is coincidental and not intended by the author.

No part of this book may be reproduced, or stored in a retrieval system, or transmitted in any form or by any means, electronic, mechanical, photocopying, recording, or otherwise, without express written permission of the publisher.

ISBN: 979-8-9924447-1-1

DEDICATION

This book is dedicated to our children and to everyone just beginning their journey. May it offer guidance as you navigate your work and inspire you to build a workplace where everyone is valued and can truly thrive. Stay true to yourself, be kind to others, and never compromise on what truly matters.

AUTHOR'S ACKNOWLEDGMENTS

I want to express my heartfelt gratitude to the illustrator of this book - not an artist by trade, but undeniably an artist at heart. With unwavering dedication, he devoted countless hours to learning, improving, and refining a new craft, each stroke a testament to his growth. Art isn't about perfection; it's about passion, about breathing life into creativity and finding joy in the process.

INTRODUCTION

Your first job can feel like a lot - new rules, expectations, and unspoken workplace norms that no one really explains to you. But don't worry, that's exactly what this book is here for! Think of it as your guide to navigating the working world, helping you avoid common mistakes and setting you up for success - without making it boring.

If someone gave you this book, take a second to thank them - they clearly want the best for you and care about your future. And if you bought it for yourself? High five! You're already ahead of the game by investing in your own success.

No matter how you got here, this book will help you tackle your first job with confidence.

Let's get started!

THE
BASICS

THE BASICS

DEFINITION:

BA·SIC

/ˈbāsik/

noun IN FORMAL

plural noun: basics

The essential facts or principles of a subject or skill.

"In this section we will cover the basics or info that you should know."

THE BASICS

SHOW UP ON TIME

This tip is important not only for work, but for life in general. Arriving on time shows that you **value** whatever it is that you are about to take part in, whether it's work, a meeting, volunteering, a party, a date, etc.

THE BASICS

BEING LATE

Unexpected things can pop up, and being late occasionally is understandable. When it happens, be sure to **inform** someone directly rather than just leaving a message. Understand your boss's preferred method of communication, whether it's a call, text, or email. Just make sure not to make being late a habit.

THE BASICS

CALLING OUT

Sometimes you'll need to call out of work, and that's okay - **life happens**, and a good boss will understand. When you do need to call out, make sure to contact your boss directly to let them know what's going on. It's important to communicate clearly and promptly. However, try not to make it a regular thing. Consistently calling out can make it seem like you're not reliable, and people are counting on you to be there.

THE *BASICS*

DRESS APPROPRIATELY

Review your company's dress code policy and stick to it. It's that **simple**.

THE BASICS

POLICIES & PROCEDURES

We get it. Reading a policy manual is pretty **boring**, but it's important to know your company's rules, especially the ones about being late, calling out, handling harassment, bullying, keeping things confidential, etc.

THE BASICS

VALUES & MISSION

It's important to understand your company's **values** and **mission** because it helps you know what the company stands for. Make sure that their values also align with your own. Trust me, you don't want to work for a company whose values conflict with yours.

THE BASICS

COMPANY CULTURE

Company culture is **Really Important!** It's basically the personality of the workplace, shaping how people interact, collaborate, and feel about their jobs. No company is perfect, but you should still aim to work for one with a positive culture. Pay attention to the culture - if it's negative, you can try to change it, but remember not to let it change you.

THE BASICS

RESPECT

Respect is treating others with kindness and consideration. It also means recognizing boundaries, being polite, and acting with integrity in your interactions with others. Everyone deserves to be treated with respect, including **YOU**!

THE BASICS

DISRESPECT

It's **NEVER** okay for anyone, including a **co-worker, boss, customer,** or even the **CEO** to be disrespectful towards you. Correcting a behavior or expressing frustration should focus on the action, not the person, and it should be done kindly and constructively.

Disrespect involves rude, belittling, or hurtful criticism that attacks the person instead of addressing the issue. If you feel like you are being disrespected, talk to your Human Resources Department or a trusted adult.

THE BASICS

INTEGRITY

Life and work will present many challenges, temptations, and chances to take the easy way out. Having integrity means being **honest** and doing the right thing, even when no one is watching.

Ultimately, integrity isn't just about your job - it's about living a life that you can be **proud** of.

THE BASICS

BEING KIND

Being kind makes it easier to build strong relationships, work as a team, and solve problems together. It also shows maturity and professionalism. **Kindness** can bridge gaps between people of different backgrounds, reduce tensions, and foster understanding.

THE BASICS

ACTIVELY LISTEN

Don't zone out when someone is talking. Actively listening means paying full **attention** to the person talking, showing that you care about what they are saying. It involves looking at them, nodding, and asking questions to make sure you understand their words and feelings.

THE BASICS

SAFETY

Your safety and the safety of your co-workers are incredibly important. If you ever feel unsafe or believe others might be at risk, it's crucial to **speak up**.

No job is worth jeopardizing your life or someone else's. Don't hesitate to voice any safety concerns you have, even if it contradicts what your boss is saying. Remember, you have the right to a **safe workplace**.

IT'S SO
PEOPLEY

IT'S SO PEOPLEY

Work is definitely going to be "peopley," and with all those people comes a mix of emotions and situations you'll need to navigate. How you handle these situations will affect you both professionally and personally. While we can't cover every possible situation you might face, we can give you some solid tips.

IT'S SO PEOPLEY

EMBRACE DIVERSITY

You can't have real progress or cool new ideas without diversity. Think about it - if everyone thought the same way, we'd be stuck in the past, and the world would never grow or change. The amazing technology, art, and solutions we have today exist because different people brought their **unique** ideas to the table.

And let's clear something up: diversity isn't a bad thing. It's not about quotas; it's about people from different backgrounds, experiences, and perspectives coming together. Diverse lives lead to diverse ideas.

At its core, diversity is about **kindness**. It's about respecting others, learning from them, and appreciating what they bring to the world. That's how we grow, connect, and make things better - for everyone.

IT'S SO PEOPLEY
IT'S OK TO DISAGREE

You won't always agree with people. However, it's important to express your opinion in a way that is **respectful** and **helpful**. Instead of arguing or criticizing, you should calmly explain your point of view, listen to the other person's perspective, and look for common ground or solutions that work for both of you.

IT'S SO PEOPLEY

CONFLICT

It would be nice to say you'll never have conflicts at work, but that's not realistic. At some point, disagreements will happen. When they do, it's important to stay respectful and **professional**, even if the other person doesn't. Try your best to listen to their concerns and work together to find a solution. If you can't work it out on your own, bring in a neutral third party to help mediate.

IT'S SO PEOPLEY

GOSSIP VS VENTING

Venting is normal. It's a way to feel heard and understood about something that happened to you. It can also be a way to decide how to remedy that situation. **Gossiping, however, is ill-intentioned and mean-spirited.**

IT'S SO PEOPLEY

LIFT OTHERS UP

You will spend a significant portion of your life at work, so take the opportunity to help **lift others up**. Share your knowledge, offer assistance, and celebrate the successes of those around you.

IT'S SO PEOPLEY

ADOPT A NEUTRAL STANCE

Instead of assuming that others are acting with good or bad intentions, try to approach situations with a **neutral mindset**. Acknowledge that you don't know the other person's motivations and try to gather more information before jumping to conclusions.

IT'S SO PEOPLEY

TEAMWORK

Teamwork is about supporting each other, solving problems together, and accomplishing more than you could alone. Remember, that each person brings unique skills, knowledge, and perspectives to the table. **Be open** to learning what other people have to say and appreciate their contributions.

IT'S SO PEOPLEY

TOXIC PEOPLE

Just like in school, work will unfortunately have some toxic people too. Toxic people often create drama, criticize or belittle others, manipulate situations, or constantly bring negativity.

Prioritize relationships that are positive, supportive, and respectful and **STAY AWAY** from the toxic people.

IT'S SO PEOPLEY

HARASSMENT & BULLYING

It's never okay to harass, bully, or make inappropriate jokes - period. No excuses, no "just kidding," no going along with it because everyone else is. If you see it happening, don't laugh it off or stay silent - speak up. Stand up for what's right and report it if needed.

And if you are the one being harassed or bullied, don't just brush it off or suffer in silence. Talk to your boss, HR, or someone who can help. You deserve to feel safe and respected at work - everyone does.

Treat people with respect, and don't let toxic behavior slide. **A great work environment starts with all of us.**

IT'S SO PEOPLEY

FRIENDSHIPS

You're going to meet a lot of awesome people at work - some of them might even turn into real friends outside of work. And that's great!

But let's be real, mixing friendship and work can get a little tricky, especially if they start slacking off.

To keep things smooth, set some **boundaries** so that your friendship doesn't mess with your working relationship.

So, if they ask you to cover for them, lie for them, or do something that breaks company rules - hard pass!

And remember, a true friend won't put you in a position that could cost you your job or hurt your reputation.

IT'S SO PEOPLEY

BOUNDARIES

Boundaries at work are a must - for yourself and others. Not everyone picks up on social cues, so if something makes you uncomfortable, speak up and be clear about it.

On the flip side, respect other people's boundaries too. **Pay attention** to social cues - like if someone's giving one-word replies or looking super busy, maybe don't linger.

Some obvious **no-go zones**? Invading personal space, spamming their inbox, blowing up their phone with texts or calls, constantly popping by their desk, or discussing controversial topics. Keeping boundaries in check helps maintain a professional and respectful environment.

IT'S SO PEOPLEY

RELATIONSHIPS AT WORK

Every company has rules about relationships, so check those first. If you're interested in someone at work, approach the relationship with **respect** and **consideration** for their boundaries. If they're not interested, accept their decision gracefully and avoid making things awkward by persisting. If you do go on a few dates and it doesn't work out, handle it maturely as well. If things do progress positively, keep it low-key at work - avoid public displays of affection and limit personal discussions to maintain professionalism.

UNDERSTANDING
EXPECTATIONS

UNDERSTANDING EXPECTATIONS

It's important to understand what's expected of you. To be completely honest, not all bosses are great at explaining that, so it might be on you to figure out what success means in your role. Being honest about what you know or don't know and asking questions can really help.

UNDERSTANDING EXPECTATIONS

ASK QUESTIONS

Don't be afraid to speak up and ask questions. Everyone learns differently, so it's **ok** to ask questions if you don't understand or need additional clarification.

UNDERSTANDING EXPECTATIONS

REPEAT IT OR WRITE IT DOWN

When learning something new, explain back the instructions to the person giving them. Write them down and, if you can, have the person giving the information review your notes. This is good for memory and making sure that you caught everything.

UNDERSTANDING EXPECTATIONS

OWN YOUR WORK

Take ownership of your work and do your tasks well. When you're assigned something, make sure you finish it on time and to the **best** of your ability. If you're unsure how to complete a task, don't hesitate to ask for help.

UNDERSTANDING EXPECTATIONS

ASK FOR HELP

Don't feel like you have to know everything. Sometimes we forget how to do things, were never trained properly, or just simply don't know the answer or process. If you don't know something, it's **ok** to admit it and ask for help.

UNDERSTANDING EXPECTATIONS

ASK FOR FEEDBACK

If you're not sure how you're doing, go ahead and ask your boss for some input. **Be specific** about what you want feedback on, like your presentation skills, writing skills, or your work on a particular project.

UNDERSTANDING EXPECTATIONS

BE OPEN TO FEEDBACK

It's important to be open to both positive and negative feedback. While it might sting a little to hear something not-so-great about yourself, feedback is meant to help you **grow** and **improve**.

UNDERSTANDING EXPECTATIONS

SPEAK UP

Don't let being new stop you from speaking up. Your thoughts, ideas, opinions, and **voice matter**. As a newcomer, you might be able to identify inefficiencies that longtime employees overlook.

Remember that there is a big difference between speaking up in a way that is helpful versus speaking up in a way that is not. How you share your ideas, thoughts, and opinions matters!

UNDERSTANDING EXPECTATIONS

BRING SOLUTIONS

It's **ok** to question why something is done a certain way. Instead of just pointing out what's wrong, think through possible solutions.

Be prepared to share your ideas and explain why you think they would work.

Don't get upset or discouraged if your idea is not implemented.

YOUR
GROWTH

YOUR GROWTH

To succeed in life and at work, growth requires extensive self-reflection and self-awareness, which can be easier said than done. It involves understanding your emotions, strengths, weaknesses, and defining who you are and who you aspire to become.

YOUR GROWTH

SELF AWARENESS

This one is a hard one, that even adults struggle with - so this will be a little longer! Self-awareness means understanding your own emotions, strengths, weaknesses, and how your actions affect others. It involves being mindful of those thoughts and feelings and recognizing how they influence **YOUR** behavior.

It's like hitting pause to check in with yourself, noticing how you're reacting to a situation, and understanding why you feel a certain way. This awareness helps you choose how to respond thoughtfully instead of just reacting automatically.

It's **not easy** because it requires an honest and sometimes uncomfortable reflection on your own thoughts, feelings, and behaviors.

YOUR GROWTH

PERSONAL GROWTH

Stay curious! Always seek ways to better yourself. Commit to learning, growing, evolving, and improving. Embrace opportunities to take on new projects and enroll in training classes. This proactive approach to personal and professional development will help you stay ahead, adapt to changes, and achieve your full potential.

YOUR GROWTH

MAKING MISTAKES

We **ALL** make mistakes. Mistakes are part of growing and learning. If you make a mistake, own up to it, apologize, and learn from it.

YOUR GROWTH

FAILING

Failure will happen, and that's okay. It's a normal part of life and a crucial part of learning and growing. **Does it suck? Yes, it does.** But failure teaches valuable lessons, helps you improve, and brings you one step closer to success. Don't be afraid of failing; instead, see it as an opportunity to become stronger and better.

YOUR GROWTH

IMPOSTER SYNDROME

At some point, you might suffer from impostor syndrome, doubting your abilities and feeling like a fraud. Remember, you've arrived at this point because of your skills and talent. You also possess the ability to keep learning and growing. Trust in your journey and the hard work you've put in. **Be confident** in your achievements and remind yourself that you belong where you are.

YOUR GROWTH

FEAR

Whether you're just starting out or are a seasoned professional, fear is a constant companion. It may arise from the unknown, the discomfort of change, or doubts about your abilities. While fear is natural and inevitable, it should **never** dictate your decisions or the path you choose.

Instead, take the time to acknowledge your fears, understand their origins, and transform them into motivation to move forward. Growth and new opportunities often lie just beyond the boundaries of fear. Embrace challenges, take calculated risks, and allow your courage to guide you toward new heights and possibilities.

YOUR GROWTH

JEALOUSY

It's natural to feel jealous at times, especially when you see others succeeding. But remember, **success is not limited** - there's plenty of it to go around, and one person's achievements don't take away from your potential. Instead of letting jealousy consume you, focus on improving your own skills and abilities.

Use others' successes as inspiration and motivation to set goals for yourself. Build connections with people who will support you and help you grow, knowing that there's room for **everyone** to thrive and succeed.

YOUR GROWTH

BE HUMBLE

Humility is a powerful trait. Being humble doesn't mean allowing others to take advantage of you. Instead, it means being open-minded, willing to listen, and eager to learn from others. A **humble attitude** allows you to acknowledge your strengths and weaknesses, accept feedback, and recognize the contributions of others.

YOUR GROWTH

YOU ARE A LEADER

No matter how long you've been at your job or what your title is, **YOU** are a leader. Yep, you read that right. Whether you realize it or not, people are watching you, depending on you, and even looking up to you. Leadership isn't just about fancy job titles - it's about how you show up and the impact you have on those around you.

Be the kind of leader you would want to follow - someone who lifts others up, leads by example, and uses their influence to **inspire**, not intimidate.

At the end of the day, leadership isn't about power - it's about people. So, **step up**, be intentional, and make your influence count in the best way possible.

YOUR GROWTH

LEARN FROM THE GREAT ONES

Take notice of the leaders you admire. What makes them great? Now, take that energy and apply it to your own actions.

During your career, you will come across incredible people and fantastic bosses, but you'll also encounter some not-so-great individuals and some seriously crappy bosses.

Learn from the great ones and model yourself after them, but don't forget to learn from the bad ones as well. Their actions and behaviors can teach you valuable lessons about how you don't want to act or lead. Use both the positive and the negative experiences to shape your own path and become the kind of person and leader you aspire to be.

SOCIAL
MEDIA

SOCIAL MEDIA

Social media can be amazing. It's a great way to connect, share, inspire, and learn, but with all the positives, there are also negatives. Like any tool, you need to be mindful of how you use it and its potential impact.

SOCIAL MEDIA

SHARING & POSTING

It's important to be **cautious** about what you share on social media, especially when it comes to your job, coworkers, or boss. Posting about work-related matters can have serious consequences, like damaging your reputation, breaching confidentiality, or even getting you into trouble with your company.

Remember, once something is online, it can be difficult to remove or control who sees it. Be mindful of what you post, and try to maintain a positive image online.

SOCIAL MEDIA

TEXTING, AUDIO MESSAGES, SNAPCHAT, TIKTOK......

Never post, share, Snapchat, or text anything that you'd be **embarrassed** about if someone else saw it. Once something's out there, you might not get the chance to explain what you really meant. Some things can't be undone and could really hurt how others see you.

SOCIAL MEDIA

TAKE A BREAK

Social media often doesn't show the full picture of reality. People post all kinds of things, and it's tempting to compare yourself to others - like where they are in their careers, the vacations they take, or what they own. **Avoid** falling into that trap. If you find yourself getting caught up in comparisons, it's okay to take a break. **Trust me**, you won't miss out on much.

WORK-LIFE
BALANCE

WORK-LIFE BALANCE

Finding a healthy work-life balance is important. Sometimes, work requires extra hours - that's normal. What's not normal is assuming that working longer hours means that you're more committed.

Prioritizing rest and boundaries leads to better performance, mental health, and job satisfaction. Smart organizations and successful people know that working smarter, not just longer, is the key to real success.

Find a balance that allows you to be productive at work while also making time for yourself, family, and loved ones. Your well-being matters, so make sure to recharge.

WORK-LIFE BALANCE

VACATION/PAID TIME OFF (PTO)

Most jobs offer vacation time or paid time off (PTO), and it's important to know what your job provides and to **USE** those days off. It's not a flex to skip vacation time, and no good boss should make you feel like you have to.

You've **earned** those days, so take them! Using your vacation time helps you relax, avoid burnout, and come back feeling refreshed. Taking care of yourself is crucial for staying happy and productive at work. So, make sure you take those breaks - **you deserve them**!

WORK-LIFE BALANCE

SICK TIME

Just like vacation time, you probably have sick time too. We're all humans, not robots, so getting sick is part of the deal. **Don't** feel guilty about using your sick days - it's a bummer that it might leave your coworkers in a tough spot, but it's way worse to show up and spread germs.

Just remember, be responsible with your sick days - don't use them just because you don't feel like going in. If you're dreading work regularly, it might be time to take a step back and figure out why.

WORK-LIFE BALANCE

BENEFITS

Make sure to **explore** the benefits that your company provides. Many employers offer health, dental, vision, life insurance, disability plans, investments, and more - all designed to support your well-being, both physically and financially.

While it may be boring or overwhelming to review these options, it's worth taking the time. If you have questions, don't hesitate to reach out to your company's benefits specialist or a trusted friend or family member who can help you understand them better.

WORK-LIFE BALANCE

PERKS

Many jobs offer **cool perks** like discounts on gyms, restaurants, or ways to earn extra money through wellness programs. Take some time to learn about all the benefits your job offers. These perks can help you stay healthy and save money, making your work experience even better. Make sure to take advantage of these opportunities to get the most out of your job!

WORK-LIFE BALANCE

401k PLANS

Two words: compound interest.

If your company offers a 401k plan and you're eligible to participate, **DO IT!** Starting to save for retirement while you're young can make a huge difference in the future. The earlier you start, the more your money can grow over time, thanks to **compound interest**. Even if retirement seems far away, contributing to a 401k now means you'll have more money when you're older and ready to retire!

WORK-LIFE BALANCE

QUITTING

Sometimes things don't work out at a job for various reasons. It could be the work itself, the people, the company culture, the benefits, the pay, or even personal reasons. No matter why you're leaving, it's important to leave on **good terms**. Always give your company the required notice. This shows professionalism and respect.

Starting out in life and your first job is a journey filled with endless growth and learning opportunities. While we couldn't possibly cover every scenario, we hope this guide has given you a solid head start. Remember, you don't need to be perfect - nobody expects it.

Instead, focus on being genuine, maintaining a strong work ethic, embracing continuous learning and personal growth, and showing kindness to those around you. These qualities will take you far!

ABOUT THE AUTHOR

Mari Orozco-Onyskin is a proud wife, mom of three amazing kids, and a devoted pet parent to two adorable fur babies.

With over 25 years of experience as an HR professional who has seen it all, Mari wrote *So, It's Your First Job* - a fun, easy-to-read guide packed with practical tips to help teens and young adults step into their first jobs with confidence. Her goal? To set them up for success and inspire a new generation to build a better, more positive work culture - one job at a time!

www.kasalearn.com

www.ingramcontent.com/pod-product-compliance
Lightning Source LLC
Chambersburg PA
CBHW052130030426
42337CB00028B/5105